WHY ME?
by
SEYMOUR
SHUBIN

WHY ME? 40 POEMS
Copyright © 2013 Seymour Shubin
All rights reserved
ISBN: 978-1-291-42305-1

10 9 8 7 6 5 4 3 2 1
First Printing

Art and Design © 2013 Steve Hussy

For all queries contact:
Murder Slim Press, 29 Alpha Road, Gorleston,
Norfolk. NR31 0LQ. United Kingdom

Murder Slim Press are:
Steve Hussy and Richard White

Published by Murder Slim Press 2013
www.murderslim.com

Printed and bound in the UK by the MPG Books Group,
Bodmin and King's Lynn

Why Me?

40 Poems

For Joe and Sydney Monte — with every good wish. Seymour Shubin

by

Seymour Shubin

Also on Murder Slim Press:

The Hunch
The Captain
Lonely No More

Also by Seymour Shubin:

Witness to Myself
The Man From Yesterday
A Matter of Fear
The Good and the Dead
My Face Among Strangers
Fury's Children
Remember Me Always
Never Quite Dead
Voices
Holy Secrets
Wellville, USA
Manta
Anyone's My Name

In memory of
Joel

--- Introduction ---
"The Art of Poetry"

Seymour Shubin -- the author of *Why Me?* -- was born in 1921 in Philadelphia. He grew up during the Great Depression and has lived through countless developments in the modern world, something the iPhone-owning Seymour refers to numerous times in this collection. Meanwhile, his writing career began with crime magazines and the bestselling *Anyone's My Name* during the detective fiction boom of the '40s and '50s, and continues now in the era of Kindle, e-readers and iPads.

The one thing that unites Seymour's career is that he has almost exclusively focussed on crime and character based stories. While you may spot his alter-ego in each of his novels, Seymour has never focussed on his own life. The closest he came to this was *Manta*, a fictionalised account of his days on a manta ray fishing boat, but even that is written in the third person.

I, no doubt along with many others, have been pestering Seymour for some time to write some sort of account of his life. The following 40 poems are the first in that vein.

The concept of *Why Me?* began with the heartfelt "Joel," which ends this finished collection. Back in 1963, Seymour's nephew, Joel Gordon Miller, a medical student, died at the tragically young age of 22 and -- in Seymour's words -- the poem seemed to write itself.

There must be something behind that. Seymour's short stories and novels speak of someone unwilling to put himself into the limelight. It seems the compact intimacy of poems allows him to come forward in a more dignified way.

This is the first -- and probably the last -- poetry collection we'll publish on Murder Slim Press. That says much about the quality of *Why Me?* but also the problems of the poetic form.

There really shouldn't be anything wrong with poetry. Think about the times people have effortlessly told you an eye-catching story or summed up their feelings profoundly. How many times have you wished that they'd write them down? Poems *can* capture great things because they are democratic. Even those who struggle with longer forms can dash down their ideas.

The problem is that poetry has always been tied to an odd "artistic" cache. The poet hides behind allusions, metaphors and whatever other literary games they can find. A simple message is hidden behind artfulness. Too often the poet writes to impress, or confuse, or shock, rather than to simply communicate. Poets write to themselves, and sink into self-gratification and self-pity.

The title *Why Me?* may indicate this collection is born out of similar regret. But while the poems are shot through with moments of sadness and loss, *Why Me?* refers much more to the wonder at having made it this far and been so happy for much of the way.

Why Me? communicates complex ideas with simplicity, honesty and skill. And, as a result, it's yet another form of writing that Seymour Shubin has mastered. What the hell will he do next?

Steve Hussy
Norfolk, 2013

Contents

Wait Your Turn 11

Half-Ball 12

Perhaps Me 14

Cod Liver Oil 15

About Lying 17

Saturday Matinee 18

My Agent, My Friend 20

Horns of Life 21

Housecalls 23

A Fish Story 24

A Coal Tale 26

Thanksgiving 27

The Hike 28

The Dummy 30

The Reunion 31

The Gunman 32

Pennsylvania Station 34

The Dancer 35

A Christmas Story 37

Night's Sleep 38

The Joke 40

The Burglary 42

Delivery Men 44

Once There Was A Truck 45

Why Me? 46

The Creek 47

Journalism 48

Manual Training 50

Phone Calls 52

The Bet 53

The Outlaws 54

Story of a Watch 56

Mischief Night 57

My Beard 59

My Partner 60

The New Car 62

Seashore in the Sun 63

Television, A Dream 65

Saturday Snow 66

Joel 68

Wait Your Turn

Where j'all go?

It's not my language, that, but it just came out.

It needs a bigger language than my own.

So many gone.

All, in fact.

The whole gang.

All the guys, and more.

Tell me, where j'all go?

And why not me?

Shh, shh.

Just wait your turn.

Half-Ball

We played what we used to call half-ball
which involves cutting a regular pimple ball in half
so you couldn't hit it too far on
a city street
or driveway,
just far enough so you could get a hit
or even a home run.

He was a gentle boy, this boy,
about two years older than the rest of us,
maybe three.
Well, he played this one game in the driveway
so full of life,
and then a neighbor came to our door the next day
with word that he'd died
and no one knew why, not even the doctors,
he just went to bed and died.
This kid with the same first name as mine,
which made it even worse,
but not as bad as when we'd drive past the cemetery
on our frequent trips to New York
to visit my eldest sister and her family,

and as we drove by I would think of him in there
with all those ghostly old people.

Then a couple of years later
they built a highway
that by-passed the cemetery.
I was glad at first
until I realized
how much more lonely he might be.

Perhaps Me

The vet said, "Are you sure?"
and Glo said yes.

But I was looking at the old girl
walking around our feet,
unknowing,
and I said let's take her home again
and see.
But Glo said it's too much of a mess.
Kind Glo who had brought Lady home
many years ago and loved her.

So we lifted the poor thing up
to the table
and she lay there, tail slapping.
And I watched the needle go in
and the poor thing's movements
stopped almost immediately.

And all I could think of was:
Why not for human suffering?
Why not for me some day?

Cod Liver Oil

When I was a kid
I used to get a nickel to drink
a tablespoon of cod liver oil
which was the most
poisonous tasting concoction
I could think of.
But a nickel was a nickel
and if you held your breath
you could get it down.

Cod liver oil was supposed
to do you great
though I was still getting occasional colds
or what they called
"Grip"
which would put you to bed for a week.

Soon my wealth was growing,
in fact the bank gave my father,
to give to me,
a small bank
where I'd put the nickels

Why Me?

until my father gave the coins to them.

But then one day my father
came home and announced
that the bank was one of many banks
that had "failed"
in the Depression
we were living in.
And my money was gone,
along with a lot of other people's money.

I never drank cod liver oil
after that.

About Lying

My mother used to say it
when I was growing up
but I never really understood it
until I was, say,
about thirteen or so.
And what she used to say was
"I hate liars,
a liar and a thief are the same."

It sounded good
though I didn't really understand it
for years,
that a liar and a thief are the same
because they both
steal
something from you.

How true, and I try to live it,
even though it puts me
at a great disadvantage.

Saturday Matinee

I think it was a dime back then
to go to a Saturday matinee.
Or was it a nickel?
Anyway, a nickel was for candy,
which you bought for a penny a piece.
I'll always remember the lady
at the store who stood so patiently
behind the counter while you decided
which "penny candy" to buy.
Indeed, when times got really tough
you got six cents worth for a nickel.

And now
with the little bag in hand
my pal Danny and I would walk fast
to the movie.
The unspoken goal
was to be first in line,
waiting for the movie
to open.
That was so important, though I don't know why,
in fact I don't think I ever got there first

and then the doors would open
and the wild rush down the aisles
to get a seat.

I always liked a corner
and I remember the screaming
and sometimes there was candy
flying in the air,
and you had to duck.
But I never threw any of mine
because there was no one I disliked enough
to give up candy.

Now to go way way back
the screams would suddenly grow louder
at the sight of a man walking down the aisle
toward the front
toward an organ.
Though someday, the rumor went
you would actually hear the actors' voices.
But who would ever believe that?

My Agent, My Friend

I got a great kick out of my picture
being in this new Danish book
among other writers being touted
as talent to watch.
But when I wrote to the editor
of the book to thank him
he said
there was no reason for the thanks,
that my book had been a good seller in Denmark.
This gave me sudden thought
because I never knew the book
had even been published in Denmark
and it immediately became clear
that my agent had pulled one on me.
Indeed he must not have told me about others,
which turned out to be the truth when I confronted him.
Though when I was leaving his office,
his eyes still wet with tears,
he said something which I don't
understand to this day:
"Here I thought you and I
were friends."

Horns of Life

It was evening and the first
of the horns could be heard
in the distance
and my brother Aaron,
barely sixteen,
was going out with a friend.
Aaron would be driving
and I'd be left alone
at home
because my parents were going out too,
and just as he was leaving
Aaron said
"Would you like to come with?"
and oh boy would I
and so I sat in back
Aaron driving,
Phil next to him.

First we went to a movie
and then for a fairly long drive
and we stopped somewhere for hot dogs,
and I loved the sound of horns in the distance,

as though announcing
the best New Years of my life.

And now of my thoughts
with Aaron long dead
and all of my friends
and I think of the horns
echoing over Aaron's grave
and I only wish
he could hear them.
Oh
if he could hear them
with me.

Housecalls

One of the things that I remember
about the Great Depression
is that all our doctors came to the house
and after they inspected me in the sick bed
the doctor and my parents would go downstairs.
And though I strained to hear
I could never make out what they were saying,
though afterward my folks would come up
to my room to assure me that it was
nothing serious
but I'd have to stay in bed
and take medicine until my fever came down.

But then one day we heard
that our doctor wouldn't be making
any more housecalls, that
you had to go to his office,
which we thought was horrible.
And we were sure his practice would dwindle
to nothing
which, when I tell it now,
gives everyone a laugh.

A Fish Story

We took our little son to a carnival,
he must have been five or six,
and we came across a game
which if you won, you won a goldfish.
I didn't want a goldfish but my son did
so I threw something
that connected
with something
and the little boy came home with a goldfish
in a water-filled plastic bag.
He was so happy and we were happy
for him.

But the next morning he came to our bed
crying.
It seems he tried to change the water
but he did it over the toilet
and the fish dropped down.
Forever lost.

The boy was crying so hard, poor thing
and so I told him that the fish

Why Me?

had made its way to the river
and was with his mother and father
and brothers and sisters
and friends,
oh yes friends.

A 60 year old lie
which I wish I could believe in now,
to meet my mother and father and sisters
and brother again
and oh yes,
all those old friends.

A Coal Tale

One of the things I used to look forward to
in the winter was when the coal truck
pulled up to our house and the "coal man"
would put a long chute, or whatever you call it,
through a basement window
and soon
the coal would go
rumbling down
into a corner.
I loved watching my father
shoveling coal
into the heater,
and lighting it,
and then at the end of the day
banking the fire
so it would last through the night.

I felt a kind of sadness when oil
replaced coal, not just in our house
but throughout the neighborhood.
Which is the height, I would think,
of sentimentality.

Thanksgiving

For years on Thanksgiving during the Depression
my mother served chicken rather
than the symbolic turkey
and I never knew why,
though the answer, I think,
was quite simple.
She didn't feel as comfortable
with turkey, which she'd never made.

Anyway, my closest friend Danny,
whose family was having
a harder time than mine,
told me one Thanksgiving that they were having
a half of a turkey.
When I told my mother
she began to cry.

Well, I'm not sure if there's
any connection
but I'll be damned if the next Thanksgiving
there was this turkey
and for every Thanksgiving after that.

The Hike

It was his fourth or fifth day in the army
in Basic Training
when word came down that they were
going on their first nighttime hike,
some said five miles, some said ten.

All he knew was that he had this bad sore throat,
the kind that if he were home
would keep him in bed for days,
maybe a whole week.
He didn't know if he had a fever
but he guessed so.
His forehead was pretty warm,
actually hot to the touch,
and he even had something
of a chill,
and there was nobody he could
tell it to.
They'd laugh at him,
or if it was the brass
they'd get angry.

Why Me?

But then a miracle happened,
it began to rain softly at first,
and then a downpour,
a flooding.
Thank God, he thought,
they would surely
cancel
it now.

Wouldn't they?
Wouldn't they?
Oh what's that?
My God, I don't believe...

The Dummy

When I was a kid
there was a class
which the kids called
the dumb class.
I never called it that
but I thought it.
It was a class of kids
in a room on the ground floor
with its own entrance into the building
who today would be thought of
as coming under Special Education.
One of the things I remember
is that nobody spoke to them,
including myself,
who actually knew one of the kids
who lived on my same block.
Didn't speak to him
until, that is, years later
when I went to buy a car
and guess
try to guess
who the dealer was.

The Reunion

He's back with family,
mother, father, sister.
The silence of the meeting
and then what we can only
imagine.
Do they touch?
Do they kiss?
Do they talk?
But do they even remember
who they were
or what they are?
Is she still his mother
and the father
with all the jokes.
Can he still tell them?
And his sister, she'd had such pain,
is she smiling again?
But do they even know
that I am
here?
I leave a stone in case they do.

The Gunman

It was the Depression, see,
and we lived next door
to them in a twin,
while they lived in a single house
that looked like a castle
to the rest of us on the block.
And they were the only people I knew
who went hunting
and twice a year they had dead deer
hanging in their yard.
And there was Tommy,
at eleven a couple of years over me,
and he had an air rifle
and it felt like it was a poor day for him
that he didn't shoot a sparrow
off a tree limb
or phone wire.

Well, this one day he and I were in the driveway
and
wouldn't you know it
there was this black bird

Why Me?

walking on the ground in front of us
and Tommy,
he handed me the gun,
and I'd never shot
anything before in my life,
but I took aim and shot
and that bird just lifted itself off the ground
and fell back.
Panicky I gave Tommy back his bee-bee gun
and ran back to my house
but what I didn't know is that a neighbor-woman
had seen the whole thing
and then kids were forbidden to play with me
for the next two weeks or so.

But that wasn't the end of it.
The kids buried the bird in the lot back there,
a funeral they never held for any of Tommy's birds
and what's more
I heard that Tommy
stood among the mourners.

Pennsylvania Station

It was a cold night in New York
and I was sitting in Pennsylvania Station
waiting for my train to Philadelphia to be announced.
Sitting close by was a shabbily dressed man
looking comfortably asleep.
One of the guards approached
and as I watched in horror
he took
one of the sleeping man's hands
and bent back one of his fingers
until the poor guy jumped awake.
"Out," the guard said, "you can't sleep here...
you gotta get out."
And the poor guy lifted himself up
and walked slowly to one of the entrances,
just about dragging his feet as he headed
out to the bitter cold.
I sat there waiting for my train
hating that son of a bitch
hating him as much as you could hate anyone
but hating myself more.

The Dancer

I saw her so many years ago
on a ship going up the Hudson River
during a school trip to West Point.
But this was before we got there
and the band was playing
and I looked into the room on the deck
and saw her dancing
and oh
what a dancer!
At one point
her partner swung her so that the back of her head
almost touched the floor.
And I remember a few days later
how, sitting in class next to her,
she asked if I would take her
to the senior prom,
I who couldn't dance a lick.
And in my shock
I made up some excuse
and hating myself,
for she was a beauty
as well as a great dancer.

Why Me?

And I even thought about it over the years
and then, finally, some sixty-five years later
in Death Notices
in the morning paper
there she is
middle-aged-looking but still a beauty.
And I wondered did she ever remember
anything of that time,
oh that time
that poor Wimpo can't forget to this day.

A Christmas Story

I used to wonder why Santa Claus
would stop next door and unload
so many toys
and then,
when he could have stopped
for just a little bit
at our house,
he would simply take off
skimming over our roof
before going way up
and then stopping at another house.

But eventually I stopped wondering
because I knew it was a matter of religion,
that he had a thing against Jewish kids.
Still, I felt a big sense of
loss
when my older brother told me
there was no Santa Claus.

Night's Sleep

Sleep is easy,
just close your eyes
and
try
not
to
think.
But if you must
think only happy ones,
like the time...
no, that wasn't happy
Think of the seashore,
the waves
think of the waves,
count them...
alright, fifty is enough.
Think of other things,
like the time
like the time.
Think of pretty things,
like...like her,
oh God, now the heart is racing,

Why Me?

nothing feels comfortable,
not this bed, the pillows,
get a drink of water
and one of the pills
just one more.
Stop kidding yourself,
you've had one,
just don't take another
mustn't take another
count...keep counting,
my God it's three o'clock,
you shouldn't have looked at your watch,
shouldn't have turned on the light and looked at it
on the night table.
Tomorrow I promise
no more pills
just the one more tonight
one more
and not tomorrow
ok, ok, this one, just this one.
Please God
don't let me
wake up dead.

The Joke

We used to play baseball on a vacant lot,
which today is covered with houses.
But this was the Great Depression
and you couldn't imagine houses there.

I played catcher,
though I didn't have a catcher's mitt,
what I had was a glove that was mostly
empty leather.
And I didn't have a mask either
or probably good sense
for I walked toward the ball
just as the batter swung
and the bat almost took my jaw away
and so I could only close my mouth
with the greatest difficulty.

After about two weeks I felt good enough
to rejoin my team,
only this time
I played the outfield.
I forgot to say that the field was large enough

for two different games at the same time,
which leads to the point of this story.

For while I manned much
of the outfield
feeling safe
in my new position
when all at once a ball from the other game
landed square on my head
hard enough to double me over
and to serve as a joke
in those gray times.

The Burglary

We were coming home
from a week's vacation,
my wife and I and our two children,
happy and with so many things
to remember.
But as we turned onto our street
we saw several police cars parked there
and we learned that two houses, including ours,
had been burglarized.

We went into our house,
disheartened,
hating the bastard
who had done this
and we began the sad business
of trying to determine what had been stolen.
I remember walking into my work room
and seeing the thick white pages of a novel
I was working on lying divided on the floor
and I gathered up the pages quickly
and eventually determined that it was all there.
But I couldn't help wonder why the thief

Why Me?

had taken it out of one of the closets
and then perhaps looked through it on the floor.
Certainly looked through it...
maybe even read parts

Which led me to wonder later on,
though telling myself I was joking,
why he hadn't taken the book with him.

Delivery Men

Sometimes I lie awake in bed
early in the morning,
too early to get up, unable
to fall back to sleep.
And I remember the clip-clop
of horse's hooves
approaching the house,
then the near-silence of the horse and wagon
stopped in front of our house
and I can picture the milkman
climbing down from the wagon
and walking up to our door
and setting down
whatever order my mother
had written for him.
Much as she did for
the iceman,
whose story is pretty much the same
though, as I say,
not quite.

Once There Was A Truck

I wish I had my father's ability
to stay calm in vexing situations.

Like the time he got a call at home
that his delivery truck -- he had a furniture business
which never attracted me --
was stuck trying to go under a bridge,
the truck being too tall for it.

My father
suggested that they
let air out of the tires
which did indeed enable the lowered truck
to back out and go another way.

A couple hours later another call came through,
which he handled remarkably well,
considering.
The truck on the drive back
was stuck under the same bridge.

Why Me?

I used to have five good buddies,
great guys all of them,
knew them from the time we were in high school.
Not that we all went to the same school
but I'm talking about
age.

Eventually we got married,
each in his time,
but still stayed close
as we got older.

And then they started falling away,
a euphemism for dying,
and guess who's left?

Why me, I sometimes wonder,
though I'm not complaining.

Really.
Honest, God.
Honest.

The Creek

There was this woods and creek
only a few blocks from where
my pal Danny and I lived
and we'd go there many times
each summer, with our lunch
in an old school bag
over our shoulders.
We'd enter a different world
cool under those trees
and the creek running swiftly,
and we'd play Tarzan
and many other games,
taking turns
who was the big guy.
But we never went swimming
because the creek wasn't clean,
which was only a technicality
and even less of one
as I look back.

Journalism

I remember how uneasy I felt when,
as graduation from high school approached,
I had to tell my parents that I wanted
to study journalism in college.
Those were the times when the best
journalism student in a prior class
had gotten a job on the biggest newspaper
in the city but, from what I'd heard,
was making only $15 a week.

I approached my parents
and was surprised that they didn't offer
even one word of objection.

As the months and then years passed
and I was working mostly as a freelancer
I never told my parents anything about the occasional
bad times I had.
Never, that is, until this one time
when I complained to my mother
about something or other.

Why Me?

She looked at me and then said something
which I didn't follow up on,
and so I never knew if she was
serious
or meant it as a joke.
What she said was:
"If I'd only known
what journalism is,
I'd never have let you take it."

Manual Training

When boys in our elementary school
reached the sixth grade
they had to take "shop" or,
to give it its classy name,
"Manual Training."

Our school did not have a room or teacher
for shop, so once a week we had to go to a nearby school.
I was worried before I even stepped into the room
for we had very few tools at home
and even less of a reason to use them,
so I was worried before I even stepped into the room.
I had reason to worry even more when I saw
the shop teacher, a woman,
who greeted us silently
and with her arms crossed.

Our first project was to take a rugged piece of wood
and plane it on one side and then the other.
but before you could leave the first side
you had to take it up to the teacher
who would determine if it was level.

Why Me?

And that was the beginning of my torture,
for as I've told my story since,
the other kids were building houses
while I was still working on the one side.

Finally
she took the wood from me
and said, "Class, class!"
and when everyone looked up,
she held up the wood and announced,
"Seymour has built a toothpick."

After she got her laugh she no longer
bothered me.
But I still have not fully stopped
killing her.

Phone Calls

When I was a kid only a
handful of people in my neighborhood
had telephones,
and one was in the drugstore.
I learned early on that if you hung around
the store without being a nuisance
and someone called and asked if
you would get this person or that
to the phone,
that person always gave you a nickel.
Or if they didn't have one on them
they would give it to you
the next time they saw you.
in the neighborhood.
All of which came to mind the other day
when I was driving through the old neighborhood
on my way to somewhere else,
looking out
at the passing world
with an iPhone in my pocket.

The Bet

I guarantee you, he said
at the end of his mother's funeral,
that the
dead will meet,
that they will look in full health
to each other,
just as they were.
Oh yeah, I thought , and
where do I collect
if you are wrong?
But that was then and this is now,
and oh how I miss her
and how I want to give
his money back.

The Outlaws

I loved my older brother,
older than me about three years.
He was in the unfortunate position
that when we got into mischief
he was the one who was
blamed.
Like that time when I was five
and we were making a racket
and finally got into one of our fights
where no one was hurt
despite all the screaming.
This night while we were
going at it
the doorbell rang and into the house
stepped the biggest policeman
I could ever remember seeing.
"Ok," he said to my brother, "let's go.
We're going to the police station."
All I remember is screaming and begging
my parents not to let the policeman take him,
for which, after making us promise to be good,
they thanked the cop and

Why Me?

undoubtedly
gave him some bills.
My brother and I couldn't have been
closer than that night.
In fact I remember crawling
into his bed.

Story of a Watch

I reached bar mitzvah age -- 13 --
in the heart of the Depression.
My father couldn't afford to give me
the usual party, so I didn't see
the usual guests or receive the usual gifts.
My parents
gave me a pen and pencil set
and one aunt -- my favorite -- said
she was going to give me
a wristwatch.
The next time I saw her I was disappointed
that she said nothing about a watch
nor did she say anything in the, yes,
years that passed.
Then one day, at a family gathering,
she came to me, a strange look on her face.
It seems someone told her the story of the watch
and she apologized awkwardly
while I found myself comforting her.
After all it was only...
it was only a watch.

Mischief Night

Halloween, when I was a kid,
was preceded by "Mischief Night."
I don't know why the community
tolerated it but I didn't question it then.

Mostly all you did was ring doorbells and run,
but sometimes
it was a lot more than that.
For instance, you'd chalk up someone's driveway
or take someone's gate
and lift it up on a garage roof.

It was all "fun," so to speak,
until the one Mischief Night
when I was preparing to go outside
but first went to answer the front doorbell.
And as I opened it
a bottle of water,
leaning against the door,
fell in and the water spread onto the rug.
"Damn kids," I shouted, but then
as I tried to calm down,

Why Me?

I knew
I wouldn't be surprised to find
one of our outside gates
on the roof of our garage...
that, almost without knowing it,
I had grown up just enough.

My Beard

When I was in elementary school
I went out for a school play for the first time.
And I was a little surprised that I got
a part, a small part but still a part.
The play took place in some eastern country
and when I told my father this
he surprised me a few days later
by giving me a beard that you hooked
onto your ears.
One of his customers was the manager
of a theater group and he'd given my father the beard.
It couldn't have been more realistic.
A few days later I wore it at rehearsal and
when the teacher saw me
her eyes widened and she asked me
for the beard and gave it to the kid
who had the lead role.
My father was furious when he heard about it
but he did nothing, afraid to cause
trouble for me.
But it was wrong, terribly wrong
to take a kid's beard.

My Partner

Some bad things happened when I was in kindergarden,
let me tell you.

One was when we were in the boys' room,
still at the urinal,
and the teacher came in and said
something like, "Let's hurry up."
Man, was I embarrassed
though just a kid.

Another wasn't my fault but she was at the piano
and we kids were sitting on the floor around her
and damn if you couldn't see under her dress,
and I mean way under.

I can pick some other things
but the one that comes to mind
took place on May Day.
Some time before that
the teacher teamed each boy up with a girl,
and believe it or not our parents were invited
while we were to do

some kind of dance around the flag pole with our partner.
Actually we were to bow to her first and sing
"Will you be my partner?" which even though I was a kid
I wished to God she'd say no.

Anyway my mother shows up and I go through it all
with maybe the strangest looking girl in the school.
In fact she was to end up in the Special Ed class,
or what we stupid kids called the Dumb Class.
I was too young to think to tell my mother
to keep this to herself.
So what seemed forever
one or another member of my family, with the exception
of my mother and father, would sing out
"Will you be my partner?"

But let me say this:
they are all gone now, and I wish...
I wish I could hear it one more time.

The New Car

My older brother and I
were ok'd by our father
to pick up the new car we
had seen and had gotten
a good price on.
But when we went to the dealer's
to pick up the car -- damn, I forget the make -- he said he'd
made a mistake and had to charge us
an additional twenty-five dollars.
He'd originally said $675, didn't he?

So in all sincerity we balked and said no-deal
until the dealer
said ok and we drove off into the
Depression night
with a brand new car,
still angry that he wanted to take us
for another twenty-five bucks.

Seashore In The Sun

Though we had a car when I was a kid
it didn't have a radio, which we didn't mind
since that seemed part of the way-off future,
if at all.
Occasionally in the summer my mother
packed food for the six of us --
mother, father, two sisters, my brother and me,
the youngest -- and we'd drive
to Atlantic City,
some 60 miles from our home.

When we got there
we went to what was called a bathhouse
where, honest to God, we would rent bathing suits
and then go out to the beach
knowing we were going to have
a hell of a sunburn if we didn't take care,
like keeping ourselves covered that first day
or even sitting under the boardwalk
for chunks of time.

But we had a great time, as always, and headed

toward home,
satisfied,
until as we drove through New Jersey
we were suddenly stopped by a cop
and my father made the mistake
of getting out of the car to argue his case.
The next I knew the cop
threw my father to the ground,
my father who never harmed anyone,
and we were all taken to a small courthouse,
where it seemed half the town looked at us
through the screen door and windows,
as if we were from the moon.

My father was fined,
but it wasn't until he went to the doctor
the next day that we learned he had
a broken arm
from having been thrown to the ground.

So it was a beautiful day gone rotten,
and we never again took a family trip
to the seashore.
And, in chilling thoughts,
it was a long time before I stopped beating up that cop.

Television, A Dream

I remember when, as kids, my friends and I
used to wonder if our radios would be replaced
some day by a fancy kind of machine
where you would actually see people's faces
and hear them talking.
It sounded so weird, so impossible,
after all
lamp-lighters
still walked many of our streets
with long poles that somehow turned the tall street lights
on and then off
in the evening.
And we still had ice delivered to our homes
on the backs of strong men,
and our mothers still scrubbed all the clothes
and then ironed them afterward.
So just that, we declared to each other,
ought to tell you we probably would never hear
a live voice on those fancy radios,
or whatever you wanted to call them.
Hell,
we'd sooner get to the moon.

Saturday Snow

There was nothing like waking up on a Saturday morning
and seeing from your bed
the white of snow on your neighbor's roof.
You went through breakfast as fast as you could
then, dragging your sled,
joined the kids
who had already gathered on a nearby hill.

After a couple hours of this a few of us
built a large igloo, scooping out the interior.
but none of us had relaxed in it yet
when Arnold came along,
a nice kid, grinning as he pulled his sled.
Tommy approached him first...
would he like to go in the igloo?
It was nice and warm in there.
Arnold said he'd love to and got on his knees
and crawled in.
And almost immediately,
despite all our hard work
Tommy slammed his shovel on the igloo,
and poor Arnold soon came crawling out covered with snow

Why Me?

while everyone
roared with laughter,
that is except for me,
who managed to hold off until later.

Joel

It came one day
fully, by itself,
without prodding, urging,
even without thought:

Does the river know the rower's
gone?
Does the rower know the
river is still here?

I've tried urging on
other things,
other thoughts,
of the long 8,
the straining,
the curve of backs,
the lifting of the shell
on strong arms...

All this and more, but it doesn't stay,
it's wrong, it doesn't say it, add to
what came only yesterday, some twenty

Why Me?

years ago,
the thing that came fully:

Does the river know the rower's gone?
Does the rower know the river is still here?

Seymour Shubin is the author of fifteen novels and more articles and short stories than he can begin to remember. His novels and stories have won numerous awards. *The Captain* received the Edgar Allan Poe Special Award from Mystery Writers of America, and was also the subject of an essay in *100 Great Detectives*. Another of his novels, *Anyone's My Name*, was a *New York Times* bestseller, and has been used as a text in university criminology courses.

Early in his career, he was managing editor of a true-crime magazine (*Official Detective Stories*) where he both wrote and edited stories. After a stint as editor of *The Psychiatric Reporter*, he finally opted to work full-time as a freelance writer.

He has previously released two books on Murder Slim Press, *The Hunch* and *Lonely No More*. *Why Me?* is his first collection of poetry.

Shubin was born and raised in Philadelphia, and is a graduate of Temple. He lives with his wife, Gloria, in one of the suburbs. They have two married children.

THE HUNCH by Seymour Shubin

"Seymour fills his books with genuine emotion and small human touches... as well as keen psychological insights. *The Hunch* is... gripping and haunting [because] the anguish and trauma that this couple go through are genuine and heartfelt."
---Dave Zeltserman (author of *Pariah*), Introduction to *The Hunch*

"Seymour Shubin is a great crime author... [and] the novel is a delight to read."
---Rod Loft, *Bookgasm*

Trade paperback size
184 pages

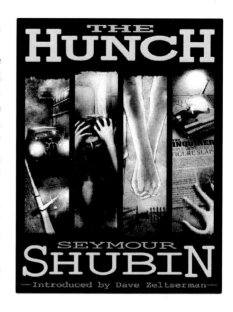

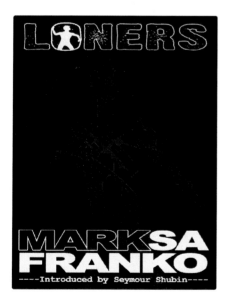

LONERS by Mark SaFranko

"Mark SaFranko dazzles with *Loners*, an addictive, wide-ranging collection of crime stories of the highest order, and some of the most compelling character-driven fiction I've read in years. Very highly recommended."
--- Jason Starr (author of *Cold Caller*)

Introduced by **Seymour Shubin** - author of *Lonely No More* and *The Hunch*
Eight pages of interior art by
Richard Watts and **Steve Hussy**

Trade paperback size
216 pages

MURDER SLIM PRESS
www.murderslim.com

HATING OLIVIA by Mark SaFranko

"The words 'raw,' 'brutal,' 'addictive'
and 'brilliant' are so overused they
have almost lost their meaning, but they
are fitting descriptions of a memoir from
a very, very talented author."
--- James Doorne, *Bizarre Magazine*

"If you're a Miller or Bukowski fan then
Hating Olivia is fresh meat, a gift tied
together with a blood-stained bow."
--- Dan Fante (author of *Mooch, Chump
Change*), Introduction to *Hating Olivia*

Trade paperback size
220 pages

LOUNGE LIZARD by Mark SaFranko

"With the publication of *Lounge Lizard* a
ground-breaking moment has occurred...
I envy the fact that you still have the
jolting, pulsating, eye-opening experience
of reading *Lounge Lizard* ahead of you."
--- Joseph Ridgwell, *Bookmunch*

"Here comes *Lounge Lizard*, a novel
written by one hardnosed, kick-ass,
American original."
--- Dan Fante (author of *Mooch, Chump
Change*), Introduction to *Lounge Lizard*

Trade paperback size
216 pages

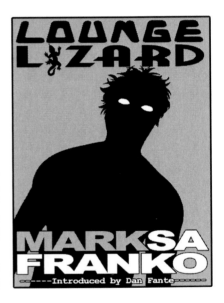

MURDER SLIM PRESS

www.murderslim.com

GOD BLESS AMERICA by Mark SaFranko

"*God Bless America* is strong stuff. Vomit, blood, piss. Guts. All delivered in scathing, acid prose. SaFranko does not spare the reader in this brutal powerhouse of a novel."
--- Mary Dearborn (author of *The Happiest Man Alive: A Biography of Henry Miller*), Introduction to *God Bless America*

"[It] is not only a passionate character study, it is also beautiful dirty realist fiction in the grand American tradition."
--- Matthew Firth, *Front and Centre*

Trade paperback size
278 pages

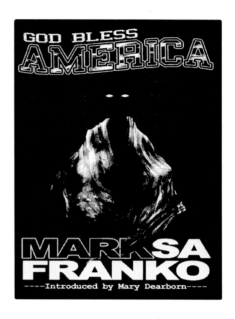

THE ANGEL by Tommy Trantino

"Tommy Trantino has given us the works - from A to TZZIT. He has put it all in one book replete with maniacal illustrations as a handbook to Eternity."
--- Henry Miller

"I haven't read a book in a long time that has hit me so hard -- a book so fierce, so poetic, so wise, so heartbreaking."
--- Howard Zinn

In print for the first time in 30 years
Introduced by Tony O'Neill
Chapbook size
92 pages

MURDER SLIM PRESS
www.murderslim.com

THE SAVAGE KICK #5
featuring:
Ivan Brunetti: Interview & Cartoons /
Another Tough Time by Mark SaFranko /
Deadly Spanking by Jim Hanley / *First*
by Steve Hussy / *Slut, Bitch, Whore* by
Julie Kazimer / Seymour Shubin:
Interview & *Lonely No More* / *Worse*
Feeling There Is by Robert McGowan /
Bloody Virtue by Jeffrey Bacon / *Carl of*
Hollyweird by Kevin O'Kendley /
Halloween by J.R. Helton / Joe R.
Lansdale: Interview & *One Of Them* /
SK's Picks of 2009 / Cover by Richard
Watts / 10 Pages of Art by Steve Hussy

Triple sized / 232 pages

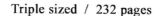

robert mcgowan

debbie drechsler

steve hussy

seymour shubin

dan fante

u.v. ray   **SK**
             # 6
             LITERARY
             MAGAZINE

2012/13

THE SAVAGE KICK #6
featuring:
Dan Fante: Interview & **Point Doom** excerpt
Dead To Rights by Seymour Shubin
The First Flower by u.v. ray
Slug by Steve Hussy
Debbie Drechsler: Interview & *Daddy Knows*
Best / *The Target* by Kevin O'Kendley
Headache by William Hart
Innocent by Aaron Garrison
Prison Prose by Jeffrey Frye
Morning by Matthew Wilding
Things That Weren't True by Rob McGowan
Savage Kick's Picks of 2010 and 2011
Cover & 12 Pages of Art by Steve Hussy

Triple sized / 206 pages

MURDER SLIM PRESS

www.murderslim.com

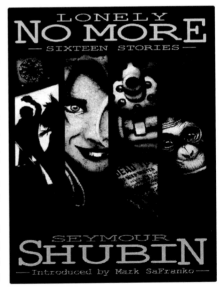